FRAMEWORK FOR INTEGRATING GENDER EQUALITY AND SOCIAL INCLUSION IN THE ASIAN DEVELOPMENT BANK'S SOUTH ASIA OPERATIONS

JULY 2023

ASIAN DEVELOPMENT BANK

ADB

CONTENTS

TABLES AND FIGURES

TABLES

FIGURES

FOREWORD BY THE VICE-PRESIDENT

The Asian Development Bank (ADB) formalized its commitment to gender equality and social inclusion (GESI) in 2004 and 2010. ADB recognizes that its operations should actively contribute to reducing poverty, inequality, and vulnerability with gender mainstreaming as a key cross-cutting strategy and social inclusion as a cross-cutting concept. ADB's Strategy 2030 reinforces this commitment by emphasizing GESI through two of its seven operational priorities: operational priority 1 is addressing remaining poverty and reducing inequalities, and operational priority 2 is accelerating progress in gender equality.

In Asia, including ADB's six developing member countries in South Asia, several significant barriers to inclusiveness impede the region's economic growth. These barriers include the following:

(i) **Gender inequality.** Gender inequality remains a major obstacle to inclusiveness in countries in South Asia and across the rest of Asia. Women often face limited access to education, employment opportunities, and decision-making positions. This gender gap in education and workforce participation leads to untapped potential and hampers economic growth by reducing overall workforce productivity.

(ii) **Social identities.** Discrimination based on religion and ethnicity creates barriers to inclusiveness and restricts disadvantaged social identity groups' access to education, employment, and social services. Their lack of access to basic services results in unequal economic participation and hinders overall development.

(iii) **Income inequality.** Widespread income disparities and wealth concentration pose significant challenges. The concentration of wealth among a few individuals or groups limits access to resources and opportunities for excluded and vulnerable groups. Income inequality undermines social mobility and can lead to social unrest, negatively impacting economic growth.

(iv) **Regional disparities.** Rural areas, remote regions, and economically disadvantaged areas often suffer from inadequate infrastructure, limited access to education and health care, and fewer job opportunities. These regional disparities can exacerbate inequality and impede inclusive growth at the national level.

The impact of these barriers on the region's economic growth is profound. When a significant portion of the population is excluded or faces limited opportunities, it results in the underutilization of human capital, reduced productivity, and stifled innovation. Moreover, social inequality can lead to social unrest, political instability, and economic uncertainty, which can negatively impact investment, trade, and overall economic development.

To contribute to achieving GESI in the region, ADB needs to identify, understand, and respond to these barriers. The responses should be in three areas:

(i) improving the collection and analysis of data on the situation of women and excluded and vulnerable groups, including the overlapping disadvantage they experience because of their intersecting disadvantaged identities;

(ii) developing the capacities of women and excluded and vulnerable groups by facilitating their economic, social, and voice empowerment; and

(iii) transforming the physical and social environment toward promoting GESI.

I commend ADB's South Asia Department for developing this GESI framework as a guide for fulfilling ADB's GESI commitments outlined in Strategy 2030 within the context of the subregion. I am confident that the framework will be instrumental in achieving GESI in the six developing member countries.

Shixin Chen
Vice-President for South, Central and West Asia

PREFACE BY THE DIRECTOR GENERAL

The Asian Development Bank (ADB) South Asia Department is pleased to present this Framework for Integrating Gender Equality and Social Inclusion in the Asian Development Bank's South Asia Operations. This framework addresses the gender equality and social inclusion (GESI) situation in our six developing member countries (DMCs) while supporting our partner government agencies' GESI policies and priority programs.

Gender inequality persists and has even worsened in South Asia and globally because of the coronavirus disease (COVID-19) pandemic, with this inequality impacting, among others, the economic, political, and social sectors, including health and education. More specifically, gender inequality has resulted in the following impacts:

(i)   Discriminatory practices, entrenched in social norms, continue to restrict women; girls; and individuals with diverse sexual orientation, gender identity and expression, and sex characteristics (SOGIESC), especially those from excluded and vulnerable groups, from accessing resources and opportunities provided by the government and external development partners.

(ii)   The intersecting factors of gender, age, disability, caste and ethnicity, diverse SOGIESC, income status, and geographic location, prevalent in many South Asian countries, contribute to multiple layers of exclusion and vulnerability for women and disadvantaged groups, hindering their ability to seize development opportunities.

(iii) Men, especially those with disabilities and those belonging to excluded social identity groups, also experience intersecting inequality, exclusion, and vulnerability. In line with the "leave no one behind" principle, development interventions must address their conditions as well. Men also play a crucial role in promoting the empowerment of women and girls, and achieving GESI.

ADB's six DMCs in South Asia have favorable laws and policy frameworks for GESI. They have robust policy commitments to protect individuals' fundamental rights, promote nondiscrimination, and safeguard the rights of various excluded and vulnerable groups. Ministries and institutional arrangements have been established and are operational in each country to implement these laws and policies. However, effective policy implementation has posed challenges across all DMCs. Many of these laws and policies do not explicitly address the overlapping disadvantages faced by women, girls, individuals with diverse SOGIESC, and other excluded and vulnerable groups. Nonetheless, the governments and civil society organizations in the six countries, alongside ADB, possess extensive experience in gender and development, and have developed exemplary practices and competencies in GESI mainstreaming. By addressing the barriers to GESI, we can leverage our collective competencies.

We hope that this GESI framework will empower South Asia Department to effectively support our partners in the six DMCs to identify, understand, and address the barriers to GESI in a context-sensitive, evidence-based, participatory, effective, and decisive manner.

K. Yokoyama

Kenichi Yokoyama
Director General, South Asia Department

ABBREVIATIONS

ADB	Asian Development Bank
CPS	country partnership strategy
CRF	corporate results framework
CSO	civil society organization
DFID	Department for International Development of the United Kingdom
DMC	developing member country
GESI	gender equality and social inclusion
LGBT	lesbian, gay, bisexual, and transgender
LGBTQI+	lesbian, gay, bisexual, transgender, queer, intersex, and others
LNOB	leave no one behind
OP	operational priority
OP1	operational priority 1
OP2	operational priority 2
RFI	results framework indicator
SARD	South Asia Department
SOGIESC	sexual orientation, gender identity and expressions, and sex characteristics
UNDP	United Nations Development Programme

I. INTRODUCTION

A. Purpose and Main Features of the Framework

1. This framework for integrating gender equality and social inclusion (GESI) in the operations of the Asian Development Bank (ADB) South Asia Department (SARD) intends to guide SARD sector divisions, resident missions, and GESI staff and consultants in fulfilling the GESI-related mandates of Strategy 2030 in South Asia. Strategy 2030 calls for the expansion of ADB's contributions to GESI. Operational priority 1 (OP1) of Strategy 2030 ("addressing remaining poverty and reducing inequalities") increases ADB's emphasis on human development, social protection, and social inclusion to ensure "that all members of society can participate in and benefit from growth."[1] Operational priority 2 (OP2) ("accelerating progress in gender equality") requires at least 75% of ADB's committed sovereign and nonsovereign operations to contribute to gender equality by 2030 along five pillars: women's economic empowerment, gender equality in human development, gender equality in decision-making and leadership, reduced women's time poverty, and women's resilience to external shocks.

2. This SARD GESI Framework is envisaged to shape the GESI operations of SARD. It evolved from an assessment of the extent and manner of integration of social inclusion in SARD operations and consultations with key stakeholders (representatives of government and civil society organizations [CSOs]) in the six developing member countries (DMCs) of ADB in South Asia in 2020–2022 (Appendix 1).[2] The assessment and consultations led to the consolidation of OP1 and OP2 in this GESI framework. This consolidation reflects SARD's view on their inextricable link and, hence, their integrated operationalization in response to the social context. More specifically, the GESI framework is based on the following conclusions:

(i) Gender inequality, which is pervasive in South Asia, intersects with other dimensions of inequality, exclusion, and vulnerability, e.g., age; disability; sexual orientation, gender identity and expressions, and sex characteristics (SOGIESC); social identity (castes, ethnic groups); income status; and geographic location. Generally, women and girls of socially excluded and vulnerable groups are the most disadvantaged, as also identified in the Strategy 2030 Operational Plan for Priority 2.[3]

(ii) The other forms of exclusion and vulnerability also intersect with each other.

---

[1] ADB. 2018. *Strategy 2030: Achieving a Prosperous, Inclusive, Resilient, and Sustainable Asia and the Pacific.* Manila. p. 14.

[2] The six DMCs of ADB in South Asia are Bangladesh, Bhutan, India, Maldives, Nepal, and Sri Lanka.

[3] Para. 43 of OP2 operational plan, which is titled "Intersectionality with other discrimination," states, "The [Sustainable Development Goal] 'leave no one behind' principle requires DMCs to address discrimination against and disadvantages for women, including those related to class, ethnicity, indigenous status, sexual orientation and gender identity, disability, religion, age, and migration... ADB will continue to identify these multiple discriminations and vulnerabilities through project poverty, social, and gender analysis." ADB. 2019. *Strategy 2030 Operational Plan for Priority 2. Accelerating Progress in Gender Equality, 2019–2024.* Manila. pp. 19–20.

3. The GESI framework is also aligned with ADB's Corporate Results Framework, 2019–2024, which provides the results framework indicators used to measure and report ADB's performance. Its level 2 results framework indicators are for the completed operations of the seven operational priorities (OPs) of Strategy 2030.[4] As most OP1 and OP2 level 2 tracking indicators are aligned with each other and mutually reinforcing (details in Appendix 2), SARD seeks to integrate their operationalization to generate more effective context-responsive interventions toward GESI results.[5] Integration means analyzing the situational context and issues from a GESI intersectional lens, designing joint plans (i.e., GESI action plan) to address GESI issues, undertaking joint monitoring and evaluation (GESI action plan progress report), and assessing and presenting their results in one report (joint assessment of GESI action plan implementation and achievements in project completion report). In SARD operations, this means expanding the practice initiated by the Nepal Resident Mission to all DMCs of ADB in South Asia.

4. The GESI framework encompasses (i) the definitions of the dimensions of gender inequality, exclusion, and vulnerability and other key terms; (ii) a guide for analyzing the barriers and opportunities to GESI and designing actions; (iii) seven key areas of action in line with ADB's GESI mainstreaming processes; and (iv) guiding principles to operationalize the key areas of action (Figure 1).

5. Overall, the SARD GESI framework seeks to identify and address the manifestations of gender inequality, disadvantage (exclusion and vulnerability), and their intersection toward achieving GESI. In brief, its components are as follows (illustrated in Figure 1 from left to right):[6]

(iii) **Dimensions of inequality, exclusion, and vulnerability and their intersectionality: Definitions of key terms**

    (a) **Excluded groups** are those who historically have been unable to fully access and/or benefit from social, economic, and political rights, opportunities, and resources because of their identities, e.g., gender; disabilities; social identities (e.g., caste, ethnicity, and religion); SOGIESC; geographic location; and income status. They experience systemic disadvantage.

    (b) **Vulnerable groups** are those who cannot access various rights, opportunities, and resources because of their situational disadvantage. People are "vulnerable" when deprivations result from a particular situation that reduces their ability to withstand shocks and access various rights, opportunities, and resources. In a person's life cycle, vulnerability is most experienced in old age and young age—especially by older people (65 and above) and disadvantaged youth. Vulnerability can also be because of climate change or disasters or migrant status. They experience situational disadvantage.

    (c) **Disadvantaged groups** (which is the preferred term—rather than excluded groups—in some DMCs) are those who historically have been unable to fully access and/or benefit from social, economic, and political rights, opportunities, and resources because of their identities (systemic disadvantage) and/or because of their vulnerability (situational disadvantage).

---

[4] ADB. 2019. *ADB Corporate Results Framework, 2019–2024: Policy Paper.* Manila.

[5] Appendix 2 presents an overview of the complementing areas of Strategy 2030 OP1 and OP2 and shows that most of the corporate results framework level 2 tracking indicators for OP1 and OP2 are aligned with each other. ADB. 2022. *Tracking Indicator Definitions.* Manila.

[6] The GESI Framework is a work in progress and will be aligned, as needed, with ADB's ongoing corporate efforts to enhance the quality of the poverty and social analyses and the results of the comprehensive review and update of its 2009 Safeguard Policy Statement (SPS).

Figure 1: South Asia Department Gender Equality and Social Inclusion Framework—An Overview

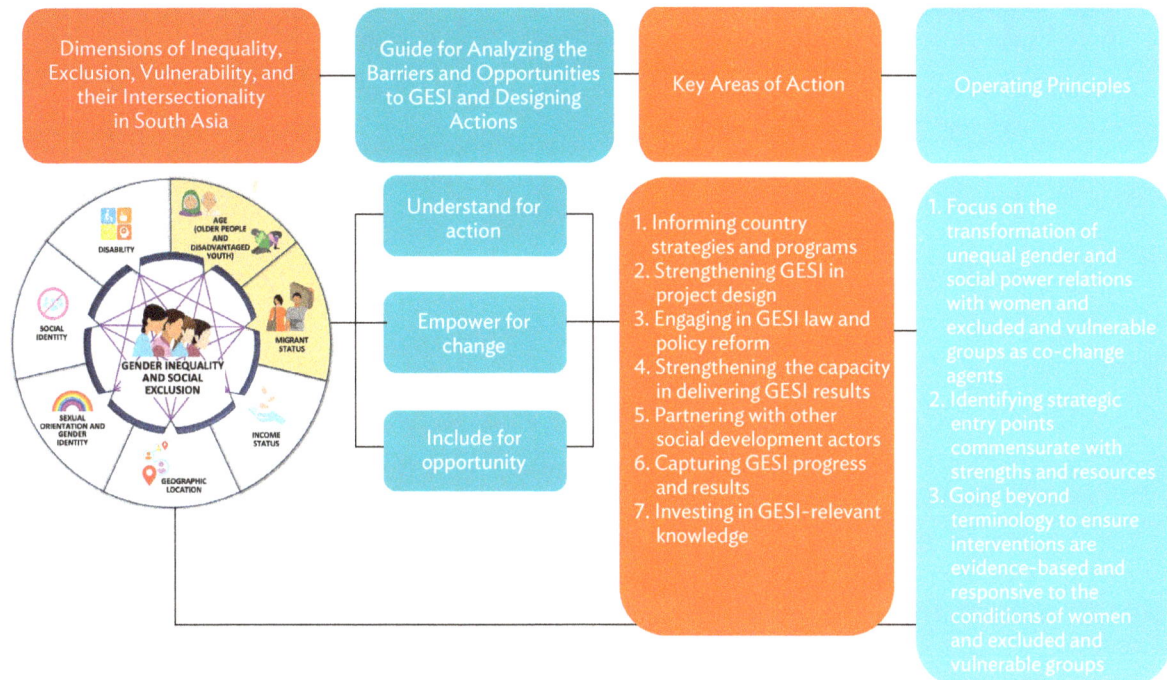

| Dimensions of Inequality, Exclusion, Vulnerability, and their Intersectionality in South Asia | Guide for Analyzing the Barriers and Opportunities to GESI and Designing Actions | Key Areas of Action | Operating Principles |

Guide column:
- Understand for action
- Empower for change
- Include for opportunity

Key Areas of Action:
1. Informing country strategies and programs
2. Strengthening GESI in project design
3. Engaging in GESI law and policy reform
4. Strengthening the capacity in delivering GESI results
5. Partnering with other social development actors
6. Capturing GESI progress and results
7. Investing in GESI-relevant knowledge

Operating Principles:
1. Focus on the transformation of unequal gender and social power relations with women and excluded and vulnerable groups as co-change agents
2. Identifying strategic entry points commensurate with strengths and resources
3. Going beyond terminology to ensure interventions are evidence-based and responsive to the conditions of women and excluded and vulnerable groups

GESI = gender equality and social inclusion.

Note: The guide for analyzing the barriers and opportunities to GESI and designing actions is patterned from the three pillars of the Leave-No-One-Behind (LNOB) Framework of the former Department for International Development of the United Kingdom (DFID), now the Foreign, Commonwealth and Development Office.

Source: Asian Development Bank South Asia Department.

(d) **Intersectionality** is an analytical lens that defines the extent of inequality, exclusion, and vulnerability (or power and advantage) that individuals or groups hold or experience by examining how their different identities intersect or overlap. An intersectional perspective is essential to show that women and girls are not homogenous groups but people experiencing different levels of disadvantage and disempowerment (or advantage and power) depending on their intersecting identities.[7] Discrimination is usually never because of one category (like gender). It is important to recognize the different sources of their discrimination. The most significant disadvantage is experienced by those who are both excluded (because of their disadvantaged identity or overlapping disadvantaged identities) and vulnerable (because

---

[7] The term intersectionality was coined by the scholar Kimberlé Crenshaw to explain the specific oppression experienced by African-American women. Thus its roots are in feminist and anti-racist theory and politics. While Black women were at the center of her analysis, the term was used to show the importance of overcoming dominant conceptions of discrimination as occurring along a single category. K. Crenshaw. 1989. Demarginalizing the Intersection of Race and Sex: A Black Feminist Critique of Antidiscrimination Doctrine, Feminist Theory and Antiracist Politics. *University of Chicago Legal Forum*. Vol. 1989, Article 8.

of their disadvantaged situation). The intersectionality lens also applies to men and boys, people with diverse SOGIESC, and other disadvantaged groups.

(e) **Gender equality** is a condition where women and men, girls and boys, and persons with diverse SOGIESC enjoy equal rights and opportunities, recognition, responsibilities, and decision-making in different spheres of society.[8]

(f) **Social inclusion** is the elimination of barriers that exclude or constrain some members of society from accessing and benefiting from social and economic services and resources and participating in their community, relationships, and decision-making.[9]

(ii) **Guide for analyzing the barriers and opportunities to GESI and designing actions:**[10]

(a) **"Understand for action.** Strengthen understanding and analysis of who, where, and why people are being left behind."

(b) **"Empower for change.** Empower those people who are furthest behind to be agents of change." In other words, enable them to engage, influence, and hold accountable the institutions that affect them. Livelihood empowerment

and mobilization empowerment (i.e., human and social capital and voice) are required for meaningful empowerment of the excluded and vulnerable people.

(c) **"Include for opportunity.** Include people who are furthest behind in development and growth processes, as well as delivering targeted programmes and services to reach populations that are particularly hard to reach." This pillar involves transforming the physical (including infrastructures, technologies, and facilities) and social environment (including social and gender norms and practices) to become sensitive to the needs of excluded and vulnerable groups.

(iii) **Key areas of action.** The results of the analysis to understand the barriers and opportunities to GESI and design responses toward empowering the excluded and vulnerable and including for opportunity will inform the execution of the seven key areas of action. Each of these key areas of action has an accompanying guidance note or tool.

(iv) **Three operating principles will guide** the key areas of action for **transformative impacts.** These principles will ensure that women and excluded and vulnerable groups are co-change agents (not passive beneficiaries) and that actions are evidence based and commensurate with the competencies and resources of SARD and partners in the six DMCs.

---

[8] This definition of gender equality covers nonbinary individuals or individuals with diverse SOGIESC in line with ADB's growing attention on their experienced vulnerability as reflected in ADB. 2021. *Safeguard Policy Statement Review and Update: Stakeholder Engagement Plan—Draft for Consultation.* Manila. p. 9 and in proposed ADB research covering 23 DMCs (including Bhutan, Nepal, and Sri Lanka) on the legal barriers to sexual orientation and gender identity inclusion.

[9] In line with the Strategy 2030 OP1 social inclusion and human development agenda, ADB has developed a disability inclusion road map to create a more systematic approach to implementing disability-inclusive development in ADB. The GESI framework will support the operationalization of this road map in South Asia. ADB. 2022. *Strengthening Disability-Inclusive Development: 2021-2025 Road Map.* Manila.

[10] This guide is an adaptation of the three pillars of the LNOB framework of the former Department for International Development of the Government of the United Kingdom (DFID) (now the Foreign, Commonwealth and Development Office)S. Herbert. 2019. *Leaving No One Behind: Perspectives and Directions from DFID Multi-Cadre Conferences. K4D Emerging Issues Report.* Brighton, United Kingdom: Institute of Development Studies. p. 15.

B. Objectives of the South Asia Department Gender Equality and Social Inclusion Framework

6. The GESI framework aims to do the following:

   (i) Provide definitions relevant to GESI and an analytical lens to examine and address gender inequality, social exclusion, and vulnerability throughout SARD operations.

   (ii) Provide guides, tools, and operating principles for integrating GESI, including women's empowerment, in different phases of SARD operations, spanning preparation of the country partnership strategy; project conceptualization, design, implementation, evaluation, and documentation; and completion.

   (iii) Contribute to the acceleration of women's empowerment, gender equality, and social inclusion in South Asia.

7. The expected outcomes of the use of the GESI framework are as follows:

   (i) Increased number of ADB-financed programs and projects with GESI features that are evidence based and address gender inequality, exclusion, vulnerability, and intersectional issues through GESI action plans and other relevant initiatives. This outcome may imply an increase in SARD investment for removing the structural barriers to GESI in the DMCs and specific sectors in South Asia.

   (ii) Improved involvement and collaboration (partnership) of SARD sector divisions, safeguards team, resident missions, and other relevant units in integrating GESI in operations and achieving GESI results.

   (iii) Increased number of ADB-financed programs and projects that report successful GESI results at completion.

II. THE SOUTH ASIA DEPARTMENT GENDER EQUALITY AND SOCIAL INCLUSION FRAMEWORK

A. The Dimensions of Gender Inequality, Exclusion, and Vulnerability in South Asia

8.   Gender inequality and other dimensions of exclusion and vulnerability, such as old age, disabilities, social identities (caste and ethnicity), SOGIESC, geographic location, and income status, persist in South Asia and demand concerted action from different stakeholders, including the government, private sector, CSOs, and multilateral development banks, such as ADB (Figure 2). The following are selected facts and figures:

  (i)   **Gender.** The United Nations Development Programme (UNDP) Human Development Report, 2021–2022 for the six DMCs in South Asia indicates that progress in women's secondary education does not ensure women's representation in Parliament or increased female labor force participation (Appendix 3).[11] The World Bank's comparison of the global female population, based on 2015 estimates, shows the female population to be 50% if data exclude India and 49% if data include India, indicating significantly fewer females in India.[12] Moreover, more than 37% of women in South Asia have experienced violence at the hands of their partners.[13] South Asia also has the highest levels of female child mortality among world regions and the highest rate of child marriage, with one in two girls getting married before the age of 18.[14]

  (ii)   **Old age.** Globally, the number of people aged 65 or older was estimated at 761 million in 2021 and is projected to increase to 1.6 billion in 2050.[15] In Sri Lanka, the older population is 1.9% higher than global estimates, with 62% women. It is projected to increase to 22.6% by 2050.[16]

---

[11]   UNDP. 2022. *Human Development Report 2021–22: Uncertain Times, Unsettled Lives: Shaping our Future in a Transforming World.* New York.

[12]   World Bank Group. 2020. *Reversals of Fortune: Poverty and Shared Prosperity 2020.* Washington, DC. Table 3B.2, p. 152.

[13]   United Nations Entity for Gender Equality and the Empowerment of Women, Asia and Pacific Regional Office. 2021. *Ending Violence against Women and Children in East Asia and Pacific: Opportunities and Challenges for Collaborative and Integrative Approaches.* Bangkok.

[14]   J.L. Solotaro and R.P. Pande. 2014. *Violence against Women and Girls: Lessons from South Asia.* Washington DC: World Bank Group.

[15]   United Nations Department of Economic and Social Affairs. 2023. *Leaving No One Behind in an Ageing World: World Social Report 2023.* New York: United Nations.

[16]   World Bank. Population Ages 65 and Above (% of Total Population). Accessed 9 May 2022.

Figure 2: Dimensions of Inequality, Exclusion, and Vulnerability in South Asia

DISABILITY

People may experience social exclusion because of physical, mental, intellectual, and sensory disability. They are considered incapable of adopting to and/or "normally" functioning in mainstream society.

SOCIAL IDENTITY

People may experience social exclusion based on their mere membership in a disadvantaged or "minority" ethnic, caste, or religious group.

SEXUAL ORIENTATION AND GENDER IDENTITY

People may experience social exclusion because of their gender expression (self-expression behavior, dress, and interaction with other people) and sexual orientation (sexual attraction toward same sex or toward both sexes).

GENDER

A woman or girl may experience social exclusion merely because of her being a woman or girl.

OLD AGE

An old person may experience vulnerability because of perceived or actual decreased physical, mental, intellectual, and sensory abilities due to age and exclusion if belonging to any excluded group.

YOUNG AGE

A disadvantaged youth may experience vulnerability due to lack of education, employment, being at risk of substance abuse and gang wars and exclusion if belonging to any excluded group.

MIGRANT STATUS

Migrants may be vulnerable to hunger, illnesses, abuses, and lack of security due to lack of resources, services, and social support. Women migrants are more vulnerable to sexual abuses.

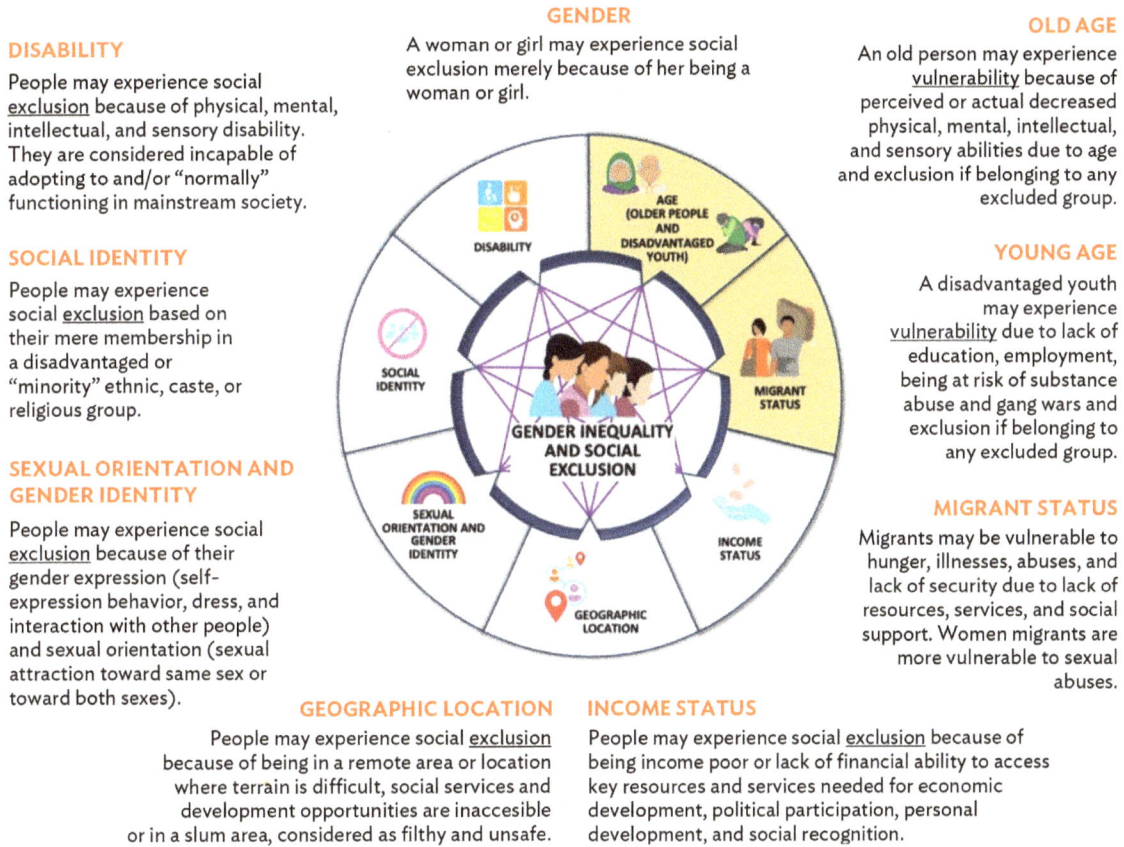

GEOGRAPHIC LOCATION

People may experience social exclusion because of being in a remote area or location where terrain is difficult, social services and development opportunities are inaccesible or in a slum area, considered as filthy and unsafe.

INCOME STATUS

People may experience social exclusion because of being income poor or lack of financial ability to access key resources and services needed for economic development, political participation, personal development, and social recognition.

Source: Consultations with representatives of governments and civil society organizations in the six developing member countries of the Asian Development Bank in South Asia in 2020–2022.

(iii) **Disability.** Long-term physical, mental, intellectual, and sensory impairments may hinder effective participation in society on an equal basis with others.[17] The world population experiencing some form of disability is 15%.[18] Disability prevalence in Maldives[19] and Sri Lanka[20] is shown at 9%. People with disabilities in Bhutan are 52% female,[21] and in India, 44%.[22]

(iv) **Sexual orientation, gender identity and expressions, and sex characteristics.** Because of a lack of representative data at the national level as well as a lack of SOGIESC questions on preexisting country-level diagnostics, there are no definitive estimates on the size of the lesbian, gay, bisexual, transgender, queer, intersex and others (LGBTQI+)[23] population in countries throughout Asia. Therefore, this

---

[17] United Nations Department of Economic and Social Affairs, Disability. 2007. *Convention on the Rights of Persons with Disabilities [A/RES/61/106]*. New York.

[18] World Health Organization. Fact Sheets: Disability.

[19] Government of Maldives, National Bureau of Statistics. *Demographic Characteristics by Disability: Household Income and Expenditure Survey 2019*. Malé.

[20] Government of Sri Lanka, Department of Census and Statistics. 2012. *Census of Population and Housing 2012*. Colombo.

[21] Government of Bhutan, National Statistics Bureau. 2018. *2017 Population and Housing Census of Bhutan: National Report*. Thimphu. p. 40.

[22] Government of India, Ministry of Statistics and Programme Implementation. 2021. *Persons with Disabilities (Divyangjan) in India – A Statistical Profile: 2021*. New Delhi. Data is based on Census 2011, which shows 14.9 million men with disabilities and 11.9 million women with disabilities.

[23] "'SOGIESC' refers to general categorizations—all people have a sexual orientation, gender identity, gender expression, and sex characteristics. 'LGBTI' refers to people who have a marginalized sexual orientation, gender identity, expression, or set of sex characteristics." M.V.L. Badgett and R. Sell. 2018. *A Set of Proposed Indicators for the LGBTI Inclusion Index*. New York: UNDP. p. 3.

document utilizes lesbian, gay, bisexual, and transgender (LGBT) population estimates from the United States as proxy data since it is one of the few countries that can use random sampling methods in nationally representative research efforts to deliver reliable population estimates. One such effort came from Gallup in 2020, which found that 5.6% of American adults (aged 18 and older) identify themselves as LGBT—5.2% as lesbian, gay, and bisexual, and 0.6% as transgender.[24] It is important to note that Gallup finds more and more people identifying as LGBT with each iteration of the research, showing that as inclusion and rights for the community increase, individuals feel more at ease to identify as LGBT in data collection efforts. Globally, the United Nations Office of the High Commissioner for Human Rights provides reliable estimates on the global size of the intersex population: 0.7%–1.7% of the entire population are born with intersex traits.[25] In Asia, estimates on the number of people with nonnormative SOGIESC exist, but this should be read with caution because of the data collection limitations and the ease at which people might identify as such. For example, there may be as many (or as few) as 10,000–50,000 transgender individuals in Bangladesh,[26] and perhaps 0.04% of the entire population in India are also third gender.[27]

In Bhutan, 316 people were registered as LGBTQI+ in 2019.[28] Although reliable population estimates don't exist, rigorous data collection from civil society, UNDP, the World Bank, and many other institutions has captured significant challenges that LGBTQI+ people experience throughout Asia, including social exclusion, violence, poverty, and more.

(v) **Geographic location.** The rural population is an estimated 80% in India. In Nepal, 52% of the rural population is female.[29] In Sri Lanka, the rural areas have a female working-age population of 51.6%.[30]

(vi) **Social identity.** In India, scheduled castes comprise 16.6% of the population (of which 48.6% are female) and scheduled tribes comprise 8.6% (of which 49.7% are female).[31] Nepal has 125 ethnic and caste groups, with female members comprising 51.5% of these groups.[32]

(vii) **Income status.** Globally, the poverty rate is at 9.2%.[33] The poverty rate in India is 21.2%, followed by Nepal at 15.0%.[34] Based on World Bank estimates, the female share of the global poor in 2018 was 51.1%, and the ratio of poor women to women in the South Asian population was almost 102.

[24] J.M. Jones. 2021. LGBT Identification Rises to 5.6% in Latest US Estimate. *Gallup*. 24 February.
[25] United Nations Office of the High Commissioner for Human Rights. Intersex People.
[26] S. Chowdhury. 2020. Transgender in Bangladesh: First School Opens for Trans Students. *BBC*. 6 November.
[27] Government of India, Ministry of Social Justice and Empowerment. 2020. *The Transgender Persons (Protection of Rights) Rules, 2020.* New Delhi.
[28] *Kuensel.* 2019. Feeling Recognised and Included. 15 June.
[29] Government of Nepal, Central Bureau of Statistics. 2012. *National Population and Housing Census 2011: National Report.* Kathmandu. Table 12, p. 39.
[30] Government of Sri Lanka, Department of Census and Statistics. 2015. *Census of Population and Housing 2012.* Battaramulla. Diagram 4.10, p.67.
[31] Office of the Registrar General and Census Commissioner, India. 2021. *Census Tables: A.10 Appendix: District wise scheduled caste population (Appendix); A.11 Appendix: District wise scheduled tribe population* (accessed 03 April 2023).
[32] Government of Nepal, Central Bureau of Statistics. 2012. *National Population and Housing Census 2011: National Report.* Kathmandu. Diagram 4.10, p. 67.
[33] World Bank. 2020. *Poverty and Shared Prosperity 2020: Reversals of Fortune.* Washington, DC. Table 1A.3: Poverty Rate at the $1.90-a-Day Poverty Line, by Economy. India's poverty rate was 21.2% in 2015–2016 and Nepal's was 15% in 2016. UNDP. 2020. *Human Development Report 2020.* New York.
[34] UNDP. 2020. *Human Development Report 2020.* New York. Table 6: Multidimensional Poverty Index: Developing Countries (Population living below $1.90 a day), p. 365.

9. Exclusion (based on gender, social identity, disability, SOGIESC, income, and geographic location) and vulnerability (based on age and migrant status) exist in each country to varying degrees. Ethnicity- or caste-based exclusion and dynamics persist in most countries. Religion-based disadvantage exists in all DMCs. Patriarchal values and social norms have kept gender inequalities alive across the region. Discriminatory practices begin before birth and affect every aspect of a person's life, especially women and excluded and vulnerable groups. Figure 3 presents an overview of the bases of exclusion existing in the DMCs, where gender inequality intersects.

Figure 3: Bases of Exclusion and Vulnerability Intersecting with Gender Inequality in South Asia

Bases of Exclusion		Bangladesh	Bhutan	India	Maldives	Nepal	Sri Lanka
OLD AGE		Financial dependency, health issues, mental health					
DISABILITIES		Considered a curse, lack of disabled-friendly infrastructure, low education, limited employment options					
SOCIAL IDENTITIES	Caste	Within Hindus		Scheduled castes, other backward classes, and denotified and nomadic tribes		Dalits	Tamils and some Sinhala groups
	Ethnicity	Tribal groups Chittagong Hill Tracts Southern plains		Pastoral communities / Scheduled tribes and particularly vulnerable tribal groups		Adivasi Janajatis, Madhesis	Sri Lankan Tamils Tamils of Indian origin
	Religion	Hindu minorities		Minority religious groups		Muslims	Christian, Hindu, and Muslim minorities
SEXUAL ORIENTATION, GENDER IDENTITY AND EXPRESSIONS, AND SEX CHARACTERISTICS		Same-sex sexual activities punishable by law	Same-sex sexual activities not punishable by law		Same-sex sexual activities punishable by law	Same-sex sexual activities not punishable by law	Same-sex sexual activities punishable by law
		Third gender legally recognized	Third gender legally recognized			Third gender legally recognized	
GEOGRAPHIC LOCATION		Rural–urban Wetlands (Haors)	Rural–urban Difficult terrain		Outer atolls Rural–urban	Rural–urban Difficult terrain	Rural–urban–estate Northern and Eastern provinces
INCOME POVERTY		Poor settlements, marginalized groups					

Note: The color codes indicate the degree of challenges: orange for a high level of challenge because of the extent of sociocultural embeddedness, yellow for a lower level of challenge, green for no formal legal exclusion, and white for not applicable. Young age (disadvantaged youth) and migrant status are not reflected in this figure as they were assessed only in some developing member countries.

Source: Consultations with representatives of governments and civil society organizations in the Asian Development Bank's six developing member countries in South Asia in 2020–2022 (Appendix 1).

10. SARD's involvement in social inclusion or OP1 builds on its commitment to gender equality in OP2. In this context, it is important to remember that in the region, the following apply:

    (i)   Gender inequality is pervasive across societies and intersects with other forms of exclusion and vulnerability (e.g., disability, social identities, SOGIESC, and old age), affecting women's lives from before birth.[35] For example, women in general and women from excluded and vulnerable groups experience social, economic, and political barriers that men of similar groups may not experience.

    (ii)   Different forms of exclusion and vulnerability intersect, affecting all the genders of the different groups. For example, men and individuals with diverse SOGIESC of excluded and vulnerable groups experience social, economic, and political barriers that men of advantaged groups may not experience.

B. The Guide for Analyzing Barriers to Gender Equity and Social Inclusion and Designing Actions: The Understand–Empower–Include Pillars

11. The responsiveness and adequacy of actions to the issues of gender inequality, exclusion, vulnerability, and their intersection depend on the quality of evidence collection and analysis methods. To inform the country partnership strategies and project designs with quality evidence and effective strategies and actions—to be reflected in the project's design and monitoring framework and GESI action plans—this framework uses the Leave-No-One-Behind (LNOB) analytical framework of the Department for International Development of the United Kingdom. The LNOB framework has three pillars: understand

for action, empower for change, and include for opportunity (Table).

12. These three pillars are further discussed in this paragraph.

    (i)   **Understand for action** is identifying barriers to GESI and analyzing the capacities of women and excluded and vulnerable groups to claim their rights and promote GESI. This analysis is necessary to understand or assess the (i) manifestations of gender and other forms of exclusion and vulnerability; (ii) factors that create or maintain social inequities based on gender, age, disability, social identity (caste, religion, ethnicity), SOGIESC, geographic location, and income; (iii) inclusiveness of formal policy, institutional frameworks, and informal norms and values; and (iv) agency of excluded and vulnerable groups. Once the root causes and mechanisms behind gender inequalities, exclusion, and vulnerability are understood, the next step is to find ways to address the identified barriers to GESI.

    (ii)   **Empower for change** is promoting the livelihood, voice, and social empowerment of women and excluded and vulnerable groups. This pillar means that sector and multisector interventions are necessary to (i) improve the assets and capacities of women and disadvantaged people through livelihood empowerment, and (ii) enhance their social capital and voice through social mobilization. For livelihood empowerment, measures (e.g., policies, systems, institutional arrangements, programs, projects, practices, and resources) will contribute to their enhanced health, education, employment, and income-earning capacities. Parallel to this is supporting them to recognize the structural causes of their situations and strengthen their sense of agency and self-determination to transform inequitable power relations.

---

[35] This echoes a statement of Naila Kabeer in her 2015 article, Gender, Poverty, and Inequality: A Brief History of Feminist Contributions in the Field of International Development, (in *Gender and Development*, 23(2). pp. 189–205) ("Gender inequality is pervasive across different groups within societies, cutting across class, race, caste, ethnicity, and other forms of inequality. It is not simply one more horizontal inequality to be added to the others. Rather, it intersects with these other inequalities in ways that intensify the disadvantages associated with other forms of inequality").

Table: Guide for Analyzing Issues and Designing Actions

Understand for Action	Empower for Change	Include for Opportunity
Purpose		
Identify barriers to GESI and analyze the capacities of women and excluded and vulnerable groups to claim their rights and promote GESI based on disaggregated data and evidence.	Promote the livelihood, voice, and social empowerment of women and excluded and vulnerable groups.	Ensure the GESI responsiveness of the social, political, and physical environment, including infrastructures, technologies, resources, and services.
Questions for Analysis		
Who are excluded and vulnerable groups?	What policies, systems, institutional arrangements, programs, projects, practices, and resources can contribute to the following?	
Why are they excluded and/or vulnerable?	Livelihood empowerment	Changing harmful and discriminatory formal and informal policies and mindsets
What are the responses to address the barriers and tap their agency and strengths?	Voice empowerment	
	Social empowerment through improving individual and collective social capital	Making public spaces and workplaces an enabling environment for GESI
		Capturing with data disaggregation and analytical evidence shifts in gender and social power relations.

GESI = gender equality and social inclusion.

Source: Asian Development Bank South Asia Department, adapted from S. Herbert. 2019. Leaving No One Behind: Perspectives and Directions from DFID Multi-Cadre Conferences. *K4D Emerging Issues Report*. Brighton, United Kingdom: Institute of Development Studies.

(iii) **Include for opportunity** is promoting the GESI-suitability of the physical environment, such as infrastructures, technologies, and spaces, and the GESI-responsiveness of the social environment, such as shifts in social and gender norms and practices, health services, educational curricula, and the political environment (e.g., governance policies, structures, and systems). This pillar means that along with empowering women and disadvantaged groups, it is important to remove and transform formal and informal institutional barriers like discriminatory legislation and institutions, deeply embedded cultural biases, and learned prejudicial social behaviors through policies, programs, and projects. The transformation should include the design of infrastructures, technologies, and facilities to make them sensitive and inclusive of women and excluded and vulnerable groups. Include for opportunity also means mobilizing the support of different sectors of society, including men and boys and advantaged groups. Engaging men is critical to women's empowerment, prevention of violence against women and girls, and gender equality. The dialogue on how toxic masculinities are learned, reinforced, practiced, and justified is critical to transforming masculinities and achieving gender equality. When men become aware of social norms that reinforce a toxic culture, they can better contribute to changing these norms into positive and healthier social values.[36] Working with people and communities with power and advantage is essential to develop their commitment to inclusive growth and belief in shared power.[37]

---

[36] ADB (Sri Lanka Resident Mission, Social Development Team). Transforming Masculinities for Women's Economic Empowerment Training Manual. Unpublished.

[37] DFID. 2010. *The Politics of Poverty: Elites, Citizens, and States*. London.

C. Seven Key Areas of Action and Supporting Guidance Notes and Tools

13. The three pillars of the LNOB framework—understand for action, empower for change, and include for opportunity—will guide the design and implementation of the seven key areas of action and their respective guidance notes and tools (Figure 4).

14. The following is a description of these key areas of action and their accompanying tools:

(i) **Key area of action 1: Informing country strategies and programs through GESI diagnostic of selected sectors** in each developing member country aims to define the GESI elements of the country partnership strategy (CPS) and country operation business plan. The GESI diagnostic of selected sectors is the main instrument for collecting and analyzing GESI issues relevant to SARD operations in DMCs. The results of this diagnostic inform the GESI features of ADB's CPSs and GESI-relevant loans, grants, and technical assistance programs and projects. To guide the execution of this first area of action is a **guidance note on conducting a GESI analysis to inform ADB's CPSs and project designs in South Asia.**

(ii) **Key area of action 2: Strengthening project design through enhancing the quality of social and gender analysis and the GESI action plan** is in line with the enhanced poverty and social analysis of the Climate Change and Sustainable Development Department. This analysis will provide evidence on who is excluded and vulnerable and the causes of their exclusion and vulnerability in project-specific sectors and areas. It will also assess the existing sector responses to identify the

strengths and areas of improvement. The guidance note for the first key area of action will also be used for this second area of action.

(iii) **Key area of action 3: Engaging DMCs at the policy level by supporting GESI-responsive policy and legal reforms** in areas relevant to SARD operations. Through policy-based loans and related technical assistance, ADB supports the improvement of the legal and policy environment in the country and sector.[38] This support ensures that proposed law and policy reforms respond to intersectional inequalities and address barriers to GESI in ADB priority sectors. GESI-related policy interventions could be related to livelihood empowerment, promotion of voice and decision-making of women and excluded and vulnerable groups, and reduction of discriminatory practices. To guide the execution of this third key area of action is a **guidance note for engaging in GESI policy dialogue and reform.**

(iv) **Key area of action 4: Developing the capacity to deliver GESI results by strengthening systems, tools, and competencies of ADB staff and executing and implementing agencies** and collaborating with the Private Sector Operations Department. The staff of ADB and executing and implementing agencies require the capacity and skills to recognize and respond to issues experienced by women and disadvantaged groups. GESI needs to be mainstreamed in institutional systems, e.g., clear GESI responsibilities in job descriptions of staff (including senior management and technical staff), women's and disadvantaged groups' significant representation in leadership structures, GESI-responsive human resource policies, and GESI-related criteria in staff performance evaluations. The organizational culture also needs to be GESI-supportive and nondiscriminatory. Guides for the execution

---

[38] ADB. 2006. *Gender, Law, and Policy in ADB Operations: A Tool Kit.* Manila.

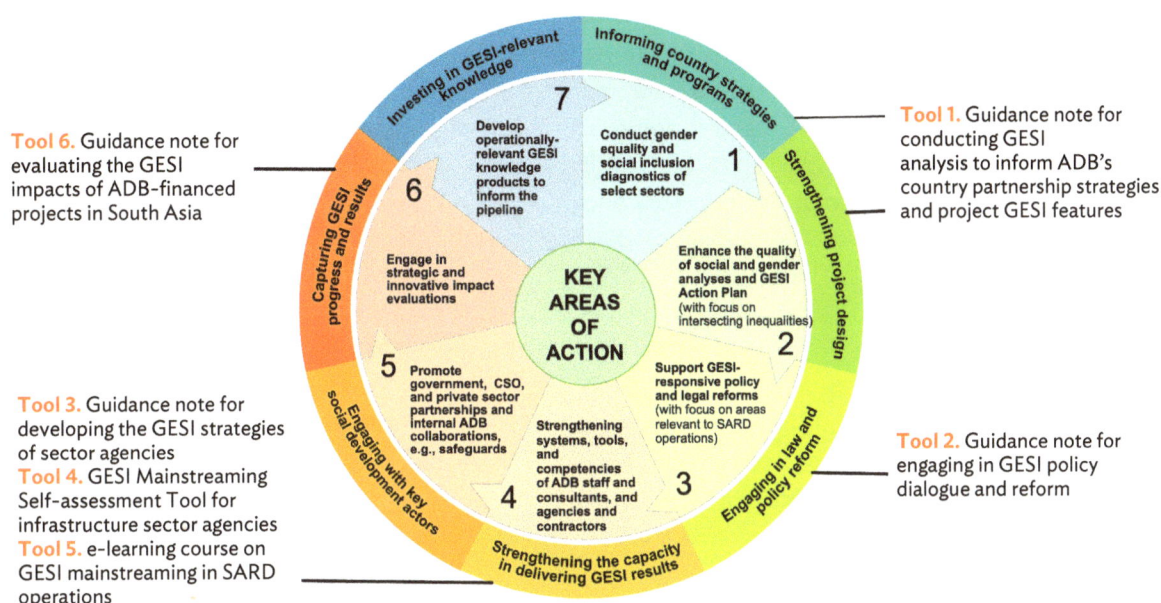

Figure 4: Gender Equality and Social Inclusion Framework Key Areas of Action and Tools

ADB = Asian Development Bank, CPS = country partnership strategy, CSO = civil society organization, GESI = gender equality and social inclusion, SARD = South Asia Department.

Source: ADB SARD.

of this fourth area of action are **the guidance note for developing the GESI strategies of sector agencies** and the **GESI mainstreaming self-assessment tool for infrastructure sector agencies.** SARD will also encourage all staff of ADB-financed projects (with and without roles in implementing the projects' GESI action plans) in South Asia to take SARD's e-learning course on the basics of GESI mainstreaming in organizations and projects in South Asia.

(v) **Key area of action 5: Partnering with other social development actors by promoting collaboration with key players and stakeholders within and outside ADB.** SARD will strengthen its partnership with governments, especially executing and implementing agencies of ADB-financed projects, in its six DMCs for GESI. It will also

engage the private sector and CSOs. ADB has followed a policy of cooperation with CSOs since 1998.[39] Working with advocacy, identity-based, and community-based CSOs is important to ensure that the voices of women and the disadvantaged are provided a platform and that their needs and priorities are identified and addressed in ADB-financed programs and projects. CSOs operate in disadvantaged communities and can contribute to the elimination of discriminatory gender and social norms. Their focus on rights-based approaches promotes transforming inequitable practices necessary for sector operations. SARD will also strengthen its strategies to empower women, girls, and people with diverse SOGIESC, and to engage men and boys for gender equality. Very important is the collaboration with other departments and units of ADB, such as the Climate Change and

---

[39] ADB. 2015. *How Does ADB Engage Civil Society Organizations in Its Operations? Findings of An Exploratory Inquiry in South Asia.* Manila.

Sustainable Development Department; NGO and Civil Society Center; Economic Research and Development Impact Department; Office of the General Counsel; Private Sector Operations Department; Culture and Talent Division; and SARD's sector divisions, safeguards team, and other units. **SARD will use the recommendations of the NGO and Civil Society Center's assessment of CSO engagement in SARD operations in 2015–2021 as a guide for this fifth area of action.**[40]

(vi) **Key area of action 6: Capturing GESI progress and results by engaging in strategic and innovative impact evaluations.** ADB requires the evaluation of all its supported completed programs and projects to assess the achievement of target outputs (as stated in the project design and monitoring framework and GESI action plan), draw lessons from approaches that worked and did not work,[41] and assess the project's contributions to ADB's corporate results framework indicators and tracking indicators. The GESI evaluation aims to capture changes in the livelihood, social, and voice empowerment of women and disadvantaged groups and the shifts in discriminatory policies and mindsets. **Informing the execution of this sixth area of action are Guidelines for the At-Exit Assessment of Gender Equality Results**

of ADB Projects[42] **and SARD's guidance note for evaluating the GESI impacts of ADB-financed projects in South Asia.** Also, SARD uses a digital GESI tracking system to monitor the progress of GESI action plan implementation.

(vii) **Key area of action 7: Investing in GESI-relevant knowledge by developing operationally relevant GESI knowledge products to inform the pipeline.** Examples of SARD's planned initiatives related to this area of action are studies on (i) the accessibility and affordability of quality care services for younger children, older persons, and people with disabilities; (ii) the economic cost of discrimination and social exclusion; (iii) GESI good practices and lessons from successful ADB-financed programs and projects (six in-country GESI results case studies); and (iv) GESI-responsive budgeting. The knowledge products also aim to document good practices in addressing the barriers to GESI and issues of intersectional inequalities experienced by women and disadvantaged groups. Some dedicated knowledge products could cover specific dimensions of exclusion and vulnerability, the effects of toxic masculinity on men and women, and lessons from engaging men and boys in promoting gender equality and women's empowerment.

[40] ADB. 2022. *Working Together for Development Results: Lessons from ADB and Civil Society Organization Engagement in South Asia.* Manila.
[41] ADB. 2016. *Guidelines for the Evaluation of Public Sector Operations.* Manila.
[42] ADB. 2022. *Guidelines for the At-Exit Assessment of Gender Equality Results of ADB Projects.* Manila.

D. Overall Operating Principles

15. The key principles that will guide the operationalization of the GESI framework (as outlined in paras. 16-19) are as follows:

(i) Focusing on Transformation

(a) Efforts to address gender inequality, social exclusion, and vulnerability should aim at transforming power relations and addressing structural discrimination. These efforts include changing uniform actions for all disadvantaged groups, such as targeting "vulnerable groups, including women," for the same activity. Uniform actions carry several risks that contradict the purpose of OP1 and OP2, i.e., to identify, analyze and address the specific needs and rights of certain social groups (and the ways they intersect). Moreover, efforts should regard women, girls, and excluded and vulnerable groups as active members of society with rights and contributions to make.

(b) The GESI framework seeks to empower excluded and vulnerable groups, transform unequal power relations in formal and informal institutions,[43] and enhance their agency. Hence, they should be involved in the transformation process as co-change agents rather than passive beneficiaries. Their collective voice is important to transforming institutions for a more equitable distribution of resources.

(ii) Identifying a Strategic Starting Point

(a) When considering the type of contribution to GESI, SARD may adopt strategic entry points that build on existing strengths and experience and are commensurate with available resources. For example, the focus on intersectional aspects of gender inequality (e.g., work on the specific constraints and needs of women and girls who live with disabilities) can serve as a strategic entry point.

(iii) Going Beyond Terminology

(a) The change of terminology from the gender action plan to the GESI action plan should lead to more evidence-based and responsive actions to explicitly address specific conditions of women and excluded and vulnerable groups in ADB's priority sectors of operations and program and project areas.

---

[43] GESI Working Group, International Development Partners Group, Nepal. 2017. *A Common Framework for Gender Equality and Social Inclusion.* Kathmandu.

III. WAY FORWARD FOR THE SOUTH ASIA DEPARTMENT

16. In moving this GESI framework forward, SARD will bear in mind the following:

    (i)   It is essential to actively promote both gender equality as well as social inclusion to ensure "no one is left behind."

    (ii) Providing adaptive solutions through adopting a GESI framework will

          (a) strengthen the approaches related to OP1 and OP2 commitments,

          (b) maintain ADB's reputation as a leader in this area, and

          (c) allow for broader policy and program dialogue with DMC partners.

    (iii) Providing technical and financial support is important to

          (a) address the intersectional inequalities experienced by women of different social profiles;

          (b) engage men and boys in the pursuit of GESI, including women's empowerment; and

          (c) support initiatives and design operations, which address specific forms of exclusion and vulnerability (e.g., people of old age, people with disabilities, people with diverse SOGIESC) in their own right.

APPENDIX 1
STAKEHOLDER CONSULTATIONS

Table A1.1: Consultations by Type of Stakeholder

Stakeholders	Participants (No.)	Women Participants (No.)	Share of Women (%)
Civil society organizations	246	129	52.44
Government	58	27	46.55
International development agencies	46	26	56.52
Key resource persons	16	9	56.25
ADB project officers	132	59	44.70
Total	**498**	**250**	**50.20**

ADB = Asian Development Bank.

Source: Report of PricewaterhouseCoopers Pvt. Ltd. (India) on the participants of stakeholder consultations on the gender equality and social inclusion (GESI) context in South Asia for the South Asia Department GESI framework.

Table A1.2: Consultations by Country and Type of Participant

Developing Member Country	Civil Society Organizations		Project Officers		Government Officers		International Development Agencies	
	Number of Consultations	Number of Participants	Number of Consultations	Number of Participants	Number of Consultations	Number of Participants	Number of Consultations	Number of Participants
Bangladesh	6	18	6	15	4	9	2	10
Bhutan	6	31	4	10	1	5	1	4
India	11	63	7	58	0	0	3	23
Maldives	7	32	5	15	8	26	2	6
Nepal	10	81	7	21	8	12	2	2
Sri Lanka	7	21	4	13	4	6	1	1
Total	**47**	**246**	**33**	**132**	**25**	**58**	**11**	**46**

Source: Report of PricewaterhouseCoopers Pvt. Ltd. (India) on the participants of stakeholder consultations on the gender equality and social inclusion (GESI) context in South Asia for the South Asia Department GESI framework.

COMPLEMENTING AREAS OF STRATEGY 2030 OPERATIONAL PRIORITIES 1 AND 2

1. Strategy 2030 operational priority 1 (OP1) and operational priority 2 (OP2) provide the underpinning premise for the gender equality and social inclusion (GESI) framework of the South Asia Department (SARD). This appendix highlights their complementing areas.

A. Operational Priority 1: Addressing Remaining Poverty And Reducing Inequalities

2. OP1 seeks to reduce multidimensional poverty and inequality in income and opportunity.[1] To achieve this objective, it employs a three-pronged strategy, representing its three pillars: (i) human capital and social protection enhanced for all, (ii) quality jobs generated, and (iii) opportunities for the most vulnerable increased. Its main target beneficiaries are poor, vulnerable, and disadvantaged people, who are described as

   - "those in the low-income bracket, women, indigenous peoples, ethnic minorities, persons with disabilities, hard-to-reach remote populations, migrants, and internally displaced and/or conflict-affected people;"[2]

   - "excluded from affordable services, such as water, sanitation, and electricity, as well as social and cultural participation, security, voice, and representation;"[3] and

   - "faced with adverse shocks, such as job loss, illness, natural hazards, or conflict [and] more likely to fall into poverty or become even poorer in the future" (footnote 2).

3. OP1 concludes that "the often overlapping nature and intersectionality of these dimensions can exacerbate vulnerability" (footnote 2). Hence, it underscores the importance of developing sector and project approaches that focus on last-mile connectivity, affordability, and vulnerability and designing projects that target the most disadvantaged.[4] As to its link to OP2, Appendix 1 of the operational plan for OP1 highlights the reduction of the gender gap and the building of resilience of women, "particularly among poor households and socially excluded groups."[5]

---

[1] ADB. 2019. *Strategy 2030 Operational Plan for Priority 1: Addressing Remaining Poverty and Reducing Inequalities, 2019–2024.* Manila.
[2] Footnote 1, p. 2, para. 4.
[3] Footnote 1, p. 1, para. 3.
[4] Footnote 1, p. 24, para. 91.
[5] Footnote 1, Appendix 1, p. 31,

4. In the ADB Corporate Results Framework (CRF), 2019–2024, at level 2 (results from completed operations), OP1 has three results framework indicators (RFIs), which are all relevant to OP2 (footnote 4 of main text):

   (i) people benefiting from improved health services, education services, or social protection (number);

   (ii) jobs generated (number); and

   (iii) poor and vulnerable people with improved standards of living (number).

5. Common to all three RFIs of OP1 is the requirement for sex disaggregation of data. The second RFI (number of jobs generated) also requires age disaggregation. The OP1 requirement of sex disaggregation will allow an analysis of the benefits for women and girls (compared to the benefits for men and boys) from completed operations, which are important to understanding the operations' outcomes on women and girls of poor, vulnerable, and disadvantaged or excluded groups.

6. In sum, OP1 benefits, which can also be found in OP2, are the following:

   (i) improved health services;

   (ii) improved education services;

   (iii) social protection, which includes social assistance, social insurance, and labor market policies and programs;

   (iv) jobs created directly under projects supported by the Asian Development Bank (ADB);

   (v) improved infrastructure services (e.g., roads constructed or upgraded, transportation systems, electricity, water and sanitation,

flood-control facilities constructed, and flood forecasting and warning system established);

   (vi) improved financial services; and

   (vii) other improvements in standards of living as set out in the design and monitoring framework.

B. Operational Priority 2: Accelerating Progress In Gender Equality

7. ADB considers the acceleration of gender equality outcomes an imperative to achieving the vision of a prosperous, inclusive, resilient, and sustainable Asia and the Pacific. Hence, under OP2, ADB commits "to support gender equality through gender-inclusive project designs in at least 75% of its sovereign and nonsovereign operations by 2030."[6] The focus of ADB's support is on five areas, which are considered the five pillars of OP2: (i) women's economic empowerment increased, (ii) gender equality in human development enhanced, (iii) gender equality in decision-making and leadership enhanced, (iv) women's time poverty and drudgery reduced, and (v) women's resilience to external shocks strengthened.

8. OP2 recognizes the issue of the intersectionality of gender-based discrimination with other forms of discrimination—thus its complementarity with OP1. The operational plan for OP2 states the following:

   "The [Sustainable Development Goal] 'leave no one behind' principle requires DMCs to address discrimination against and disadvantages for women, including those related to class, ethnicity, indigenous status, sexual orientation and gender identity, disability, religion, age, and migration.

---

[6] ADB. 2019. *Strategy 2030 Operational Plan for Priority 2. Accelerating Progress in Gender Equality, 2019–2024.* Manila. p. 1, para. 1.

Women, among the vulnerable and poor households affected by climate change and disaster impacts, economic shocks, and involuntary resettlement, may also require special attention. ADB will continue to identify these multiple discriminations and vulnerabilities through project poverty, social, and gender analysis."[7]

9. In the ADB CRF, 2019–2024, at level 2 (results from completed operations), OP2 has five RFIs, which are also within the mandates of OP1:

    (i) skilled jobs for women generated (number);

    (ii) women and girls completing secondary and tertiary education and/or other training (number);

    (iii) women represented in decision-making structures and processes (number);

    (iv) women and girls with increased time savings (number); and

    (v) women and girls with increased resilience to climate change, disasters, and other external shocks (number).

C. Further Complementing Areas and Relation of Operational Priorities 1 and 2

10. A document on the tracking indicators of ADB's CRF, 2019–2024 shows 8 of 9 OP1 tracking indicators aligned with 11 of 15 tracking indicators of OP2 (Table).[8]

11. While highlighting the complementing indicators of OP1 and OP2, SARD continues to be committed to OP1 and OP2 performance indicators in the ADB CRF, 2019–2024 that are not in the above table. Separate analyses and action plans may be necessary for these indicators or targets, which are as follows:

    (i) OP1 distinct tracking indicator, not aligned with but relevant to OP2: 1.2.3 Total number of new and/or improved policies and standards related to physical working conditions and social protection developed and implemented under ADB-supported projects

    (ii) OP2 distinct tracking indicators, not aligned with any OP1 indicators

        (a) 2.2.3 Total number of solutions under ADB projects to prevent or address gender-based violence

        (b) 2.3.1 Total number of women whose leadership capacity improved under the ADB project's capacity-building initiatives

        (c) 2.4.2 Total number of child and elderly care services established or improved under ADB projects

        (d) 2.5.1 Total number of community initiatives that build the resilience of women and girls against external shocks under ADB projects

12. In linking the complementing areas of OP1 and OP2, this SARD GESI framework brings to the fore and prioritizes the empowerment needs of the most disadvantaged members of excluded and vulnerable groups—women, girls, and people with diverse SOGIESC.

---

[7] Footnote 6, pp. 19–20, para. 43.
[8] ADB. 2022. *Tracking Indicator Definitions*. Manila.

Table A2: Aligned Operational Priorities 1 and 2 Tracking Indicators (Corporate Results Framework Indicators Level 2)

No.	Operational Priority 1 Tracking Indicators	Operational Priority 2 Tracking Indicators
1	1.1.1 Total number of individuals enrolled in improved education and/or training under ADB projects, sex disaggregated	2.2.1 Total number of female students enrolled in STEM or nontraditional TVET, both full-time and part-time, under ADB projects
2	1.1.2 Total number of health services established and improved under ADB projects	2.2.2 Total number of health services benefiting women and girls established or improved under ADB projects
3	1.1.3 Total number of social protection schemes established or improved under ADB projects (includes social assistance, social insurance, and labor market programs)	2.5.3 Total number of savings and insurance schemes and initiatives for women implemented or established under ADB projects 2.5.4 Total number of social schemes for women and girls implemented or established under ADB projects
4	1.2. Number of jobs created directly under ADB-supported projects, age and sex disaggregated 1.2.1 Business development and finance sector measures supported in implementation	2.1 Total number of skilled jobs created for women through direct employment under ADB projects 2.1.1 Total number of female students enrolled in TVET and other job training, both full-time and part-time, under ADB projects
5	1.3.2 Total number of new financial products and services made available to the poor and vulnerable under ADB projects	2.1.2 Total number of women who open new bank accounts (regardless of amount, type of account, or purpose of account opening) over the course of ADB projects
6	1.2.2 Total number of models for business development and financing established or improved with ADB support	2.1.3 Number of women-owned or -led SMEs end borrowers, or if not available, the number of women-owned or -led loan accounts opened (regardless of amount) over the course of the project
7	1.3.2 Total number of infrastructure assets aimed at increased use by the poor and vulnerable established or improved under ADB projects • roads constructed or upgraded • transportation systems • electricity, water, and sanitation • flood-control facilities constructed, and flood forecasting and warning system established • digital infrastructure • other improved services as set out in the DMF	2.1.4 Total number of women and girls who benefit from project offering new or improved infrastructure under ADB projects • new or improved water supply by women and girls • new or improved sanitation by women and girls • new or improved transport by women and girls • new or improved electricity connection (via energy distribution) by women and girls • other improved infrastructure by women and girls as set out in the DMF and/or GAP 2.4.1 Total number of time-saving or gender-responsive assets and/or services provided under ADB projects • safe and adequate number of toilets for women • separate sections or carriages for women in trains or buses • private breastfeeding corners or rooms in public areas • Safe sidewalks for pedestrians • better lighting on streets and in stations on streets • other relevant designs as set out in the DMF and/or GAP 2.5.2 Total number of climate and disaster-resilient infrastructure assets and/or services that benefit women and girls established or improved under ADB projects • flood-control systems • protective embankments

continued on next page

Table A2 *continued*

No.	Operational Priority 1 Tracking Indicators	Operational Priority 2 Tracking Indicators
		• seawall rehabilitation • retrofitting of buildings • risk-sensitive planning, hazard mapping, ecosystem-based management, and disaster risk financing • other relevant assets and services as set out in the DMF and/or GAP.
8	1.3.3 Total number of measures for increased inclusiveness supported in implementation	2.3.2 Total number of measures on gender equality supported in implementation. Measures refer to laws, regulatory or legislative frameworks, strategies, or policies

ADB = Asian Development Bank; DMF = design and monitoring framework; GAP = gender action plan; SMEs = small and medium-sized enterprises; STEM = science, technology, engineering, and mathematics; TVET = technical and vocational education and training.

Source: ADB. 2022. *Tracking Indicator Definitions*. Manila.

APPENDIX 3
GENDER INEQUALITIES IN SOUTH ASIA

Country	Gender Inequality Index Rank		SDG3.1 Maternal mortality ratio (deaths per 100,000 live births)	SDG3.7 Adolescent birth rate (births per 1,000 women ages 15-19)	SDG4.6 Population with at least some secondary education (% ages 25 and older)		SDG5.5 Share (%) of seats in parliament held by women	Labor force participation rate (% ages 15 and older)	
	Value	Rank (of 189 countries)			Female	Male		Male	Female
	2021	2021	2017	2021	2021	2021	2021	2021	2021
Bangladesh	0.530	131	173	75.5	50.6	58.5	20.9	34.9	78.8
Bhutan	0.415	98	183	19.0	23.6	32.3	16.7	51.6	67.4
India	0.490	122	133	17.2	41.8	53.8	13.4	19.2	70.1
Maldives	0.348	83	53	73	46.4	41.5	4.6	34.3	67.5
Nepal	0.452	113	186	63.8	28.8	44.7	33.6	78.7	80.8
Sri Lanka	0.383	92	36	15.7	84.0	84.2	5.4	30.9	68.5

SDG = Sustainable Development Goal.

Source: United Nations Development Programme. 2022. *Human Development Report 2021–22: Uncertain Times, Unsettled Lives: Shaping our Future in a Transforming World.* New York.